P9-EEU-653

DATE DUE

JUL 01 2010	

The Trouble with Poetry and Other Poems

Nine Horses

Sailing Alone Around the Room

Picnic, Lightning

The Art of Drowning

Questions About Angels

The Apple That Astonished Paris

Poetry 180: A Turning Back to Poetry (editor)

180 More: Extraordinary Poems for Every Day (editor)

Ballistics

Ballistics

poems

Billy Collins

RANDOM HOUSE NEW YORK

Published in the United States by Random House, an imprint of The Random House Publishing Group, a division of Random House, Inc., New York.

RANDOM HOUSE and colophon are registered trademarks of Random House, Inc.

Previous publication information about some of the poems contained within this work can be found beginning on page 111.

Library of Congress Cataloging-in-Publication Data
Collins, Billy.
Ballistics : poems / Billy Collins.
p.   cm.
ISBN 978-1-4000-6491-5
I. Title.
PS3553.O47478B35 2008
811'.54—dc22

Printed in the United States of America on acid-free paper

www.atrandom.com

9 8 7 6 5 4 3 2 1

First Edition

Book design by Liz Cosgrove

For Chris Calhoun
advocate and pal

Even as a cow she was lovely.

     —Ovid, *Metamorphoses*

contents

three

four

Ballistics

August in Paris

I have stopped here on the rue des Écoles
just off the boulevard St-Germain
to look over the shoulder of a man
in a flannel shirt and a straw hat
who has set up an easel and a canvas chair
on the sidewalk in order to paint from a droll angle
a side-view of the Church of Saint Thomas Aquinas.

But where are you, reader,
who have not paused in your walk
to look over my shoulder
to see what I am jotting in this notebook?

Alone in this city,
I sometimes wonder what you look like,
if you are wearing a flannel shirt
or a wraparound blue skirt held together by a pin.

But every time I turn around
you have fled through a crease in the air
to a quiet room where the shutters are closed
against the heat of the afternoon,
where there is only the sound of your breathing
and every so often, the turning of a page.

one

Brightly Colored Boats Upturned
on the Banks of the Charles

What is there to say about them
that has not been said in the title?
I saw them near dawn from a glassy room
on the other side of that river,
which flowed from some hidden spring
to the sea; but that is getting away from
the brightly colored boats upturned
on the banks of the Charles,
the sleek racing sculls of a college crew team.

They were beautiful in the clear early light—
red, yellow, blue and green—
is all I wanted to say about them,
although for the rest of the day
I pictured a lighter version of myself
calling time through a little megaphone,
first to the months of the year,
then to the twelve apostles, all grimacing
as they leaned and pulled on the long wooden oars.

Searching

I recall someone once admitting
that all he remembered of *Anna Karenina*
was something about a picnic basket,

and now, after consuming a book
devoted to the subject of Barcelona—
its people, its history, its complex architecture—

all I remember is the mention
of an albino gorilla, the inhabitant of a park
where the Citadel of the Bourbons once stood.

The sheer paleness of him looms over
all the notable names and dates
as the evening strollers stop before him

and point to show their children.
These locals called him Snowflake,
and here he has been mentioned again in print

in the hope of keeping his pallid flame alive
and helping him, despite his name, to endure
in this poem where he has found another cage.

Oh, Snowflake,
I had no interest in the capital of Catalonia—
its people, its history, its complex architecture—

no, you were the reason
I kept my light on late into the night
turning all those pages, searching for you everywhere.

High

On that clear October morning,
I was only behind a double espresso
and a single hit of anti-depressant,

yet there, on the shore of the reservoir
with its flipped-over rowboats,
I felt like I was walking with Jane Austen

to borrow the jargon of the streets.
Yes, I was wearing the crown,
as the drug addicts like to say,

knitting a bonnet for Charlie,
entertaining the troops,
sitting in the study with H. G. Wells—

so many ways to express that mood
of royal goodwill
when the gift of sight is cause enough for jubilation.

And later in the afternoon
when I finally came down,
a lexicon was waiting for me there, too.

In my upholstered chair by a window
with dusk pouring into the room,
I appeared to be doing nothing,

but inside I was busy riding the marble,
as the lurkers like to put it,
talking to Marco Polo,

juggling turtles,
going through the spin cycle,
or—my favorite, if I had to have one—out of milk.

The Four-Moon Planet

> I have envied the four-moon planet.
>
> —*The Notebooks of Robert Frost*

Maybe he was thinking of the song
"What a Little Moonlight Can Do"
and became curious about
what a lot of moonlight might be capable of.

But wouldn't this be too much of a good thing?
and what if you couldn't tell them apart
and they always rose together
like pale quadruplets entering a living room?

Yes, there would be enough light
to read a book or write a letter at midnight,
and if you drank enough tequila
you might see eight of them roving brightly above.

But think of the two lovers on a beach,
his arm around her bare shoulder,
thrilled at how close they were feeling tonight
while he gazed at one moon and she another.

Evasive Maneuvers

I grew up hiding from the other children.
I would break off from the pack
on its patrol of the streets every Saturday

and end up alone behind a hedge
or down a dim hallway in a strange basement.
No one ever came looking for me,
which only added to the excitement.

I used to hide from adults, too,
mostly behind my mother's long coat
or her floral dress depending on the season.

I tried to learn how to walk
between my father's steps while he walked
like the trick poodle I had seen on television.

And I hid behind books,
usually one of the volumes of the encyclopedia
that was kept behind glass in a bookcase,
the letters of the alphabet in gold.

Before I knew how to read,
I sat in an armchair in the living room
and turned the pages, without a clue

about the worlds that were pressed
between D and F, M and O, W and Z.

Maybe this explains why
I looked out the bedroom window
first thing this morning
at the heavy trees, low gray clouds,

and said the word *gastropod* out loud,
and having no idea what it meant
went downstairs and looked it up
then hid in the woods from my wife and our dog.

August

The first one to rise on a Sunday morning,
I enter the white bathroom
trying not to think of Christ or Wallace Stevens.

It's before dawn and the road is quiet,
even the birds are silent in the heat.
And standing on the tile floor,

I open a little nut of time
and nod to the cold water faucet,
with its chilled beaded surface

for cooling my wrists and cleansing my face,
and I offer some thanks
to the electricity swirling in the lightbulbs

for showing me the toothbrush and the bottle of
	aspirin.
I went to grammar school for Jesus
and to graduate school for Wallace Stevens.

But right now, I want to consider
only the water and the light,
always ready to flow and spark at my touch,

and beyond the wonders of this white room—
the reservoir high in the mountains,
the shore crowded with trees,

and the dynamo housed in a colossus of brick,
its bright interior, and up there,
a workman smoking alone on a catwalk.

The Poems of Others

Is there no end to it
the way they keep popping up in magazines
then congregate in the drafty orphanage of a book?

You would think the elm would speak up,
but like the dawn it only inspires—then more of them
    appear.
Not even the government can put a stop to it.

Just this morning, one approached me like a possum,
snout twitching, impossible to ignore.
Another looked out of the water at me like an otter.

How can anyone dismiss them
when they dangle from the eaves of houses
and throw themselves in our paths?

Perhaps I am being harsh, even ridiculous.
It could have been the day at the zoo
that put me this way—all the children by the cages—

as if only my poems had the right to exist
and people would come down from the hills
in the evening to view them in rooms of white marble.

So I will take the advice of the mentors
and put this in a drawer for a week
maybe even a year or two and then have a calmer
       look at it—

but for now I am going to take a walk
through this nearly silent neighborhood
that is my winter resting place, my hibernaculum,

and get my mind off the poems of others
even as they peer down from the trees
or bark at my passing in the guise of local dogs.

Aubade

If I lived across the street from myself
and I was sitting in the dark
on the edge of the bed
at five o'clock in the morning,

I might be wondering what the light
was doing on in my study at this hour,
yet here I am at my desk
in the study wondering the very same thing.

I know I did not have to rise so early
to cut open with a penknife
the bundles of papers at a newsstand
as the man across the street might be thinking.

Clearly, I am not a farmer or a milkman.
And I am not the man across the street
who sits in the dark because sleep
is his mother and he is one of her many orphans.

Maybe I am awake just to listen
to the faint, high-pitched ringing
of tungsten in the single lightbulb
which sounds like the rustling of trees.

Or is it my job simply to sit as still
as the glass of water on the night table
of the man across the street,
as still as the photograph of my wife in a frame?

But there's the first bird to deliver his call,
and there's the reason I am up—
to catch the three-note song of that bird
and now to wait with him for some reply.

No Things

This love for the petty things,
part natural from the slow eye of childhood,
part a literary affectation,

this attention to the morning flower
and later in the day to a fly
strolling along the rim of a wineglass—

are we just avoiding the one true destiny,
when we do that? averting our eyes from
Philip Larkin who waits for us in an undertaker's coat?

The leafless branches against the sky
will not save anyone from the infinity of death,
nor will the sugar bowl or the sugar spoon on the table.

So why bother with the checkerboard lighthouse?
Why waste time on the sparrow,
or the wildflowers along the roadside

when we should all be alone in our rooms
throwing ourselves against the wall of life
and the opposite wall of death,

the door locked behind us
as we hurl ourselves at the question of meaning,
and the enigma of our origins?

What good is the firefly,
the droplet running along the green leaf,
or even the bar of soap spinning around the bathtub

when ultimately we are meant to be
banging away on the mystery
as hard as we can and to hell with the neighbors?

banging away on nothingness itself,
some with their foreheads,
others with the maul of sense, the raised jawbone of
    poetry.

The First Night

> The worst thing about death must be
> the first night.
>
> —Juan Ramón Jiménez

Before I opened you, Jiménez,
it never occurred to me that day and night
would continue to circle each other in the ring of death,

but now you have me wondering
if there will also be a sun and a moon
and will the dead gather to watch them rise and set

then repair, each soul alone,
to some ghastly equivalent of a bed.
Or will the first night be the only night,

a darkness for which we have no other name?
How feeble our vocabulary in the face of death,
how impossible to write it down.

This is where language will stop,
the horse we have ridden all our lives
rearing up at the edge of a dizzying cliff.

The word that was in the beginning
and the word that was made flesh—
those and all the other words will cease.

Even now, reading you on this trellised porch,
how can I describe a sun that will shine after death?
But it is enough to frighten me

into paying more attention to the world's day-moon,
to sunlight bright on water
or fragmented in a grove of trees,

and to look more closely here at these small leaves,
these sentinel thorns,
whose employment it is to guard the rose.

January in Paris

Poems are never completed—they are
only abandoned.

—Paul Valéry

That winter I had nothing to do
but tend the kettle in my shuttered room
on the top floor of a pensione near a cemetery,

but I would sometimes descend the stairs,
unlock my bicycle, and pedal along the cold city streets
often turning from a wide boulevard
down a narrow side street
bearing the name of an obscure patriot.

I followed a few private rules,
never crossing a bridge without stopping
mid-point to lean my bike on the railing
and observe the flow of the river below
as I tried to better understand the French.

In my pale coat and my Basque cap
I pedaled past the windows of a patisserie
or sat up tall in the seat, arms folded,
and clicked downhill filling my nose with winter air.

I would see beggars and street cleaners
in their bright uniforms, and sometimes
I would see the poems of Valéry,
the ones he never finished but abandoned,
wandering the streets of the city half-clothed.

Most of them needed only a final line
or two, a little verbal flourish at the end,
but whenever I approached,
they would retreat from their makeshift fires
into the shadows—thin specters of incompletion,

forsaken for so many long decades
how could they ever trust another man with a pen?

I came across the one I wanted to tell you about
sitting with a glass of rosé at a café table—
beautiful, emaciated, unfinished,
cruelly abandoned with a flick of panache

by Monsieur Paul Valéry himself,
big fish in the school of Symbolism
and for a time, president of the Committee of Arts and
     Letters
of the League of Nations if you please.

Never mind how I got her out of the café,
past the concierge and up the flights of stairs—
remember that Paris is the capital of public kissing.

And never mind the holding and the pressing.
It is enough to know that I moved my pen
in such a way as to bring her to completion,

a simple, final stanza, which ended,
as this poem will, with the image
of a gorgeous orphan lying on a rumpled bed,
her large eyes closed,
a painting of cows in a valley over her head,

and off to the side, me in a window seat
blowing smoke from a cigarette at dawn.

two

Ballistics

When I came across the high-speed photograph
of a bullet that had just pierced a book—
the pages exploding with the velocity—

I forgot all about the marvels of photography
and began to wonder which book
the photographer had selected for the shot.

Many novels sprang to mind
including those of Raymond Chandler
where an extra bullet would hardly be noticed.

Nonfiction offered too many choices—
a history of Scottish lighthouses,
a biography of Joan of Arc and so forth.

Or it could be an anthology of medieval literature,
the bullet having just beheaded Sir Gawain
and scattered the band of assorted pilgrims.

But later, as I was drifting off to sleep,
I realized that the executed book
was a recent collection of poems written

by someone of whom I was not fond
and that the bullet must have passed through
his writing with little resistance

at twenty-eight hundred feet per second,
through the poems about his childhood
and the ones about the dreary state of the world,

and then through the author's photograph,
through the beard, the round glasses,
and that special poet's hat he loves to wear.

Pornography

In this sentimental painting of rustic life,
a rosy-cheeked fellow
in a broad hat and ballooning green pants

is twirling a peasant girl in a red frock
while a boy is playing a squeeze-box
near a turned-over barrel

upon which rest a knife, a jug, and a small drinking
    glass.
Two men in rough jackets
are playing cards at a wooden table.

And in the background a woman in a bonnet
stands behind the half-open Dutch door
talking to a merchant or a beggar who is leaning on a
    cane.

This is all I need to inject me with desire,
to fill me with the urge to lie down with you,
or someone very much like you,

on a cool marble floor or any fairly flat surface
as clouds go flying by
and the rustle of tall leafy trees

mixes with the notes of birdsong—
so clearly does the work speak of vanishing time,
obsolete musical instruments,

passing fancies, and the corpse
of the largely forgotten painter moldering
somewhere beneath the surface of present-day France.

Greek and Roman Statuary

The tip of the nose seemed the first to be lost,
then the arms and legs,
and later the stone penis if such a thing were featured.

And often an entire head followed the nose
as it might have done when bread
was baking in the side streets of ancient Rome.

No hope for the flute once attached
to the lips of that satyr with the puffed-out cheeks,
nor for the staff the shepherd boy once leaned on,

the sword no longer gripped by the warrior,
the poor lost ears of the sleeping boy,
and whatever it was Aphrodite once held in her severed
    hand.

But the torso is another story—
middle man, the last to go, bluntly surviving,
propped up on a pedestal with a length of pipe,

and the mighty stone ass endures,
so smooth and fundamental, no one
hesitates to leave the group and walk behind to stare.

And that is the way it goes here
in the diffused light from the translucent roof,
one missing extremity after another—

digits that got too close to the slicer of time,
hands snapped off by the clock,
whole limbs caught in the mortal thresher.

But outside on the city streets,
it is raining, and the pavement shines
with the crisscross traffic of living bodies—

hundreds of noses still intact,
arms swinging and hands grasping,
the skin still warm and foreheads glistening.

It's anyone's guess when the day will come
when there is nothing left of us
but the bare, solid plinth we once stood upon

now exposed to the open air,
just the wind in the trees and the shadows
of clouds sweeping over its hard marble surface.

Quiet

It occurred to me around dusk
after I had lit three candles
and was pouring myself a glass of wine
that I had not uttered a word to a soul all day.

Alone in the house,
I was busy pushing the wheel in a mill of paper
or staring down a dark well of ink—
no callers at the door, no ring of the telephone.

But as the path lights came on,
I did recall having words with a turtle
on my morning walk, a sudden greeting
that sent him off his log splashing into the lake.

I had also spoken to the goldfish
as I tossed a handful of pellets into their pond,
and I had a short chat with the dog,
who cocked her head this way and that

as I explained that dinner was hours away
and that she should lie down by the door.
I also talked to myself as I was typing
and later on while I looked around for my boots.

So I had barely set foot on the path
that leads to the great villa of silence
where men and women pace while counting beads.
In fact, I had only a single afternoon

of total silence to show for myself,
a spring day in a cell in Big Sur,
twenty or so monks also silent in their nearby cells—
a community of Cameldolites,

an order so stringent, my guide told me,
that they make the Benedictines,
whom they had broken away from in the 11th century,
look like a bunch of Hells Angels.

Out of a lifetime of running my mouth
and leaning on the horn of the ego,
only a single afternoon of being truly quiet
on a high cliff with the Pacific spread out below,

but as I listened to the birdsong
by the window that day, I could feel my droplet
of silence swelling on the faucet
then dropping into the zinc basin of their serenity.

Yet since then—
nothing but the racket of self-advertisement,
the clamor of noisy restaurants,
the classroom proclamations,

the little king of the voice having its say,
and today the pride of writing this down,
which must be the reason my pen
has turned its back on me to hide its face in its hands.

Scenes of Hell

We did not have the benefit of a guide,
no crone to lead us off the common path,
no ancient to point the way with a staff,

but there were badlands to cross,
rivers of fire and blackened peaks,
and eventually we could look down and see

the jeweler running around a gold ring,
the boss trapped in an hourglass,
the baker buried up to his eyes in flour,

the banker plummeting on a coin,
the teacher disappearing into a blackboard,
and the grocer silent under a pyramid of vegetables.

We saw the pilot nose-diving
and the whore impaled on a bedpost,
the pharmacist wandering in a stupor

and the child with toy wheels for legs.
You pointed to the soldier
who was dancing with his empty uniform

and I remarked on the blind tourist.
But what truly caught our attention
was the scene in the long mirror of ice:

you lighting the wick on your head,
me blowing on the final spark,
and our children trying to crawl away from their
    eggshells.

Hippos on Holiday

is not really the title of a movie
but if it was I would be sure to see it.
I love their short legs and big heads,
the whole hippo look.
Hundreds of them would frolic
in the mud of a wide, slow-moving river,
and I would eat my popcorn
in the dark of a neighborhood theater.
When they opened their enormous mouths
lined with big stubby teeth
I would drink my enormous Coke.

I would be both in my seat
and in the water playing with the hippos,
which is the way it is
with a truly great movie.
Only a mean-spirited reviewer
would ask on holiday from what?

Carpe Diem

Maybe it was the fast-moving clouds
or the spring flowers quivering among the dead leaves,
but I knew this was one day I was born to seize—

not just another card in the deck of the year,
but March 19th itself,
looking as clear and fresh as the ten of diamonds.

Living life to the fullest is the only way,
I thought as I sat by a tall window
and tapped my pencil on the dome of a glass
    paperweight.

To drain the cup of life to the dregs
was a piece of irresistible advice,
I averred as I checked someone's dates

in the *Dictionary of National Biography*
and later, as I scribbled a few words
on the back of a picture postcard.

Crashing through the iron gates of life
is what it is all about,
I decided as I lay down on the carpet,

locked my hands behind my head,
and considered how unique this day was
and how different I was from the men

of hari-kari for whom it is disgraceful
to end up lying on your back.
Better, they think, to be found facedown

in blood-soaked shirt
than to be discovered with lifeless eyes
fixed on the elegant teak ceiling above you,

and now I can almost hear the silence
of the temple bells and the lighter silence
of the birds hiding in the darkness of a hedge.

Lost

There was no art in losing that coin
you gave me for luck, the one with the profile
of an emperor on one side and a palm on the other.

It rode for days in a pocket
of my black pants, the paint-speckled ones,
past storefronts, gas stations and playgrounds,

and then it was gone, as lost as the lost
theorems of Pythagoras, or the *Medea* by Ovid,
which also slipped through the bars of time,

and as ungraspable as the sin that landed him—
forever out of favor with Augustus—
on a cold rock on the coast of the Black Sea,

where eventually he died, but not before
writing a poem about the fish of those waters,
into which, as we know, he was never transformed,

nor into a flower, a tree, or a stream,
nor into a star like Julius Caesar,
not even into a small bird that could wing it back to
    Rome.

Dublin

So much to be learned out here in the drizzle
with all the tall busses swinging themselves
so close to me around corners and men
in bunches smoking outside the betting parlors.

And when the rain falls steadily enough
to drive me into a gallery or a city castle,
then the knowledge only comes pouring down
whether I am in the mood for it or not.

Today, it's the codex of Leonardo on display
in the dim light where you touch a screen
to turn a page, the margins busy with pulleys
and siphons, whirlwinds, tides, and sluices.

And better informed I am to read on a little card
the news that Herbert Hoover translated
into English for the first time the works
of Agricola, the father of modern mineralogy himself.

Out the windows of the gallery,
a jumble of raincoats and black umbrellas,
and so my afternoon education continues
with the discovery in a vitrine of Vegetarius,

who in the 4th century came up
with the idea of underwater warfare,
hand-to-hand combat beneath the lily pads
as if bloodying one another on the ground were not
    enough.

And if his illustration of an armed soldier
standing on the bottom of a lake
and breathing through a snake-like tube
comes at me tonight and shakes me out of sleep,

I will not coax an oval pill from its bottle
nor put on a robe and stand by the stove
looking at the ads in a magazine
while some milk is heating in a pan.

I only need to slide into place
the image of Leonardo at a table by a window,
his marvelling head resting in his hands,
as he wonders if water could exist on the moon.

New Year's Day

Everyone has two birthdays
according to the English essayist Charles Lamb,
the day you were born and New Year's Day—

a droll observation to mull over
as I wait for the tea water to boil in a kitchen
that is being transformed by the morning light
into one of those brilliant rooms of Matisse.

"No one ever regarded the First of January
with indifference," writes Lamb,
for unlike Groundhog Day or the feast of the
  Annunciation,

this one marks nothing but the passage of time,
I realized, as I lowered a tin diving bell
of tea leaves into a little body of roiling water.

I admit to regarding my own birthday
as the joyous anniversary of my existence
probably because I was, and remain
to this day in late December, an only child.

And as an only child—
a tea-sipping, toast-nibbling only child
in a colorful room this morning—
I would welcome an extra birthday,
one more opportunity to stop what we are doing
for a moment and reflect on my being here on earth.

And one more might be a small consolation
to us all for having to face a death-day, too,
an X in a square
on some kitchen calendar of the future,

the day when each of us is thrown off the train of time
by a burly, heartless conductor
as it roars through the months and years,

party hats, candles, confetti, and horoscopes
billowing up in the turbulent storm of its wake.

The Day Lassie Died

It is 5:40 in Sawyer County, Wisconsin, a Tuesday
a few days before the birthday of Martin Luther, yes
it is 1959 and I need to do my chores
which include milking the ten cows—
did I mention it was 5:40 in the morning?—
and driving them with a stick into the pasture.

After breakfast (I am thinking oatmeal
with brown sugar and some raisins)
I will drive the twelve miles into town
and pick up a few things,

a tin of hoof softener for the horse,
some batteries, shells, a pair of rubber gloves,
and something for my wife but I don't know what.
Maybe this cotton apron
with little pictures of the Eiffel Tower on it,

or she might like some hairpins, a box of tissues,
yet I am tempted by this anthology
of the Cavalier poets edited by Thomas Crofts
or maybe *The Pictorial History of Eton College* by B.J.W. Hill,

but after pacing up and down the aisles
of Olsen's Emporium, I finally settle on
The Zen Teaching of Huang Po
translated from the Chinese (obviously)
by John Blofeld and published
recently by the infamous Grove Press,

and when I take everything up to Henry
at the big bronze cash register,
he asks have you seen today's *Sentinel*
and there's her face, the dark eyes,
the long near-smile, and the flowing golden coat

and I'm leaning on the barn door back home
while my own collie, who looks a lot like her,
lies curled outside in a sunny patch
and all you can hear as the morning warms up
is the sound of the cows' heavy breathing.

three

Tension

Never use the word *suddenly* just to create
tension.

—*Writing Fiction*

Suddenly, you were planting some yellow petunias
outside in the garden,
and suddenly I was in the study
looking up the word *oligarchy* for the thirty-seventh
time.

When suddenly, without warning,
you planted the last petunia in the flat,
and I suddenly closed the dictionary
now that I was reminded of that vile form of
governance.

A moment later, we found ourselves
standing suddenly in the kitchen
where you suddenly opened a can of cat food
and I just as suddenly watched you doing that.

I observed a window of leafy activity
and beyond that, a bird perched on the edge
of the stone birdbath
when suddenly you announced you were leaving

to pick up a few things at the market
and I stunned you by impulsively
pointing out that we were getting low on butter
and another case of wine would not be a bad idea.

Who could tell what the next moment would hold?
another drip from the faucet?
another little spasm of the second hand?
Would the painting of a bowl of pears continue

to hang on the wall from that nail?
Would the heavy anthologies remain on their shelves?
Would the stove hold its position?
Suddenly, it was anyone's guess.

The sun rose ever higher in the sky.
The state capitals remained motionless on the wall map
when suddenly I found myself lying on a couch
where I closed my eyes and without any warning

began to picture the Andes, of all places,
and a path that led over the mountains to another
    country
with strange customs and eye-catching hats,
each one suddenly fringed with colorful little tassels.

The Golden Years

All I do these drawn-out days
is sit in my kitchen at Pheasant Ridge
where there are no pheasants to be seen
and last time I looked, no ridge.

I could drive over to Quail Falls
and spend the day there playing bridge,
but the lack of a falls and the absence of quail
would only remind me of Pheasant Ridge.

I know a widow at Fox Run
and another with a condo at Smokey Ledge.
One of them smokes, and neither can run,
so I'll stick to the pledge I made to Midge.

Who frightened the fox and bulldozed the ledge?
I ask in my kitchen at Pheasant Ridge.

Vermont, Early November

It was in between seasons,
after the thin twitter of late autumn
but before the icy authority of winter,

and I took in the scene from a porch,
a tableau of silo and weathervane
and a crowd of ferns on the edge of the woods—

nothing worth writing about really,
but it is too late to stop now
that the ferns and the silo have been mentioned.

I drank my warm coffee
and took note of the disused tractor
and the lopsided sign to the cheese factory.

Not one of those mornings
that makes you want to seize the day,
not even enough glory in it to make you want

to grasp every other day,
yet after staring for a while
at the plowed-under fields and the sky,

I turned back to the order of the kitchen
determined to seize firmly
the second Wednesday of every month that lay ahead.

The Effort

Would anyone care to join me
in flicking a few pebbles in the direction
of teachers who are fond of asking the question:
"What is the poet trying to say?"

as if Thomas Hardy and Emily Dickinson
had struggled but ultimately failed in their efforts—
inarticulate wretches that they were,
biting their pens and staring out the window for a clue.

Yes, it seems that Whitman, Amy Lowell
and the rest could only try and fail,
but we in Mrs. Parker's third-period English class
here at Springfield High will succeed

with the help of these study questions
in saying what the poor poet could not,
and we will get all this done before
that orgy of egg salad and tuna fish known as lunch.

Tonight, however, I am the one trying
to say what it is this absence means,
the two of us sleeping and waking under different roofs.
The image of this vase of cut flowers,

not from our garden, is no help.
And the same goes for the single plate,
the solitary lamp, and the weather that presses its face
against these new windows—the drizzle and the
        morning frost.

So I will leave it up to Mrs. Parker,
who is tapping a piece of chalk against the blackboard,
and her students—a few with their hands up,
others slouching with their caps on backwards—

to figure out what it is I am trying to say
about this place where I find myself
and to do it before the noon bell rings
and that whirlwind of meatloaf is unleashed.

The Lamps Unlit

It is difficult to write an aubade,
a song about noon, or a few crepuscular lines
without stopping to realize
just where you are on the dial of a certain day,

which is at least a beginning
and better than the usual blind rush
into the future, believed to reside
over the next in an infinite series of hills.

I'm all for noticing that the light
in the tops of the trees
is different now with the grass moist
and cold, the heads of flowers yet unfolded,

all for occupying a chair by a window
or a wayside bench for an hour—
time enough to look here and there
as the caravan of time crosses the sand,

time to think of the dead and lost friends,
their faces hidden in the foliage,
and to consider the ruination of love,
a wisp of smoke rising from a chimney.

And who cares if it takes me all day
to write a poem about the dawn
and I finish in the dark with the night—
some love it best—draped across my shoulders.

China

I am an ant inside a blue bowl
on the table of a cruel prince.

Battle plans are being discussed.
Much rice wine is poured.

But even when he angers
and drives a long knife into the table,

I continue to circle the bowl,
hand-painted with oranges and green vines.

Looking Forward

Whenever I stare into the future,
the low, blue hills of the future,
shading my eyes with one hand,

I no longer see a city of opals
with a sunny river running through it
or a dark city of coal and gutters.

Nor do I see children
donning their apocalyptic goggles
and hiding in doorways.

All I see is me attending your burial
or you attending mine,
depending on who gets to go first.

There is a light rain.
A figure under an umbrella
is reading from a thick book with a black cover.

And a passing cemetery worker
has cut the engine to his backhoe
and is taking a drink from a bottle of water.

(detail)

It was getting late in the year,
the sky had been low and overcast for days,
and I was drinking tea in a glassy room
with a woman without children,
a gate through which no one had entered the world.

She was turning the pages of a large book
on a coffee table, even though we were drinking tea,
a book of colorful paintings—
a landscape, a portrait, a still life,
a field, a face, a pear and a knife, all turning on the
    table.

Men had entered the gate, but no boy or girl
had ever come out, I was thinking oddly
as she stopped at a page of clouds
aloft in a pale sky, tinged with red and gold.
This one is my favorite, she said,

even though it was only a detail, a corner
of a larger painting which she had never seen.
Nor did she want to see the countryside below
or the portrayal of some myth
in order for the billowing clouds to seem complete.

This was enough, this fraction of the whole,
just as the leafy scene in the windows was enough
now that the light was growing dim,
as was she enough, perfectly by herself
somewhere in the enormous mural of the world.

Le Chien

I remember late one night in Paris
speaking at length to a dog in English
about the future of American culture.

No wonder she kept cocking her head
as I went on about "summer movies"
and the intolerable poetry of my compatriots.

I was standing and she was sitting
on a dim street in front of a butcher shop,
and come to think of it, she could have been waiting

for the early morning return of the lambs
and the bleeding sides of beef
to their hooks in the window.

For my part, I had mixed my drinks,
trading in the tulip of wine
for the sharp nettles of whiskey.

Why else would I be wasting my time
and hers trying to explain "corn dog,"
"white walls," and "the March of Dimes"?

She showed such patience for a dog
without breeding while I went on—
in a whisper now after shouts from a window—

about "helmet laws" and "tag sale"
wishing I only had my camera
so I could carry a picture of her home with me.

On the loopy way back to my hotel—
after some long and formal goodbyes—
I kept thinking how I would have loved

to hang her picture over the mantel
where my maternal grandmother
now looks down from her height as always,

silently complaining about the choice of the frame.
Then, before dinner each evening
I could stand before the image of that very dog,

a glass of wine in hand,
submitting all of my troubles and petitions
to the court of her dark-brown, adoring eyes.

Addendum

What I forgot to tell you in that last poem
if you were paying attention at all
was that I really did love her at the time.

The maritime light in the final lines
might have seemed contrived,
as false as any puffed up Italian sonnet,

and the same could be said
for the high cliffside flowers
I claimed to have introduced to her hair

and sure, the many imaginary moons
I said were circling our bed as we slept,
the cosmos enclosed by the walls of the room.

But the truth is we loved
to take long walks on the windy shore,
not the shore between the sea of her

and the symbolic land of me,
but the real shore of empty shells,
the sun rising, the water running up and back.

On the Death of a Next-Door Neighbor

So much younger and with a tall, young son
in the house above ours on a hill,
it seemed that death had blundered once again.

Was it poor directions, the blurring rain,
or the too-small numerals on the mailbox
that sent his dark car up the wrong winding driveway?

Surely, it was me he was looking for—
overripe, childless, gaudy with appetite,
the one who should be ghosting over the rooftops

not standing barefooted in this kitchen
on a sun-shot October morning
after eight days and nights of downpour,

me with my presumptuous breathing,
my arrogant need for coffee,
my love of the colorful leaves beyond the windows.

The weight of my clothes, not his,
might be hanging in the darkness of a closet today,
my rake idle, my pen across a notebook.

The harmony of this house, not his,
might be missing a voice,
the hallways jumpy with the cry of the telephone—

if only death had consulted his cracked leather map,
then bent to wipe the fog
from the windshield with an empty sleeve.

Separation

With only a two-and-a-half-inch wooden goose
to keep me company at this desk,
I am beginning a new life of discipline.

No more wandering out in thunderstorms
hoping to be hit by a bolt of lightning
from the raised hand of Randall Jarrell.

No more standing at an open window
with my lyre strings finely tuned
waiting for a stray zephyr to blow my way.

Instead I will report here every morning
and bend over my work like St. Jerome
with his cowl, quill, and a skull for a paperweight.

And the small white goose with his yellow
feet and beak and a black dot for an eye
is more than enough companionship for me.

He is well worth the dollar I paid for him
in a roadside trinket shop in New Mexico
and more familiar to me than the household deities

of this guest cottage in the woods—
two porcelain sphinxes on the mantel
and a pale, blank-eyed Roman bust on a high shelf

on this first morning without you—
me holding a coffee I forgot to pay for
and the gods of wind and sun contending in the
    crowded trees.

four

Adage

When it's late at night and branches
are banging against the windows,
you might think that love is just a matter

of leaping out of the frying pan of yourself
into the fire of someone else,
but it's a little more complicated than that.

It's more like trading the two birds
who might be hiding in that bush
for the one you are not holding in your hand.

A wise man once said that love
was like forcing a horse to drink
but then everyone stopped thinking of him as wise.

Let us be clear about something.
Love is not as simple as getting up
on the wrong side of the bed wearing the emperor's clothes.

No, it's more like the way the pen
feels after it has defeated the sword.
It's a little like the penny saved or the nine dropped
    stitches.

You look at me through the halo of the last candle
and tell me love is an ill wind
that has no turning, a road that blows no good,

but I am here to remind you,
as our shadows tremble on the walls,
that love is the early bird who is better late than never.

The Flight of the Statues

The ancient Greeks . . . used to chain their
statues to prevent them from fleeing.

—Michael Kimmelman

It might have been the darkening sky
that sent them running in all directions
that afternoon as the air turned a pale yellow,

but were they not used to standing out
in the squares of our city
in every kind of imaginable weather?

Maybe they were frightened by a headline
on a newspaper that was blowing by
or was it the children in their martial arts uniforms?

Did they finally learn about the humans
they stood for as they pointed a sword at a cloud?
Did they know something we did not?

Whatever the cause, no one will forget
the sight of all the white marble figures
leaping from their pedestals and rushing away.

In the parks, the guitarists fell silent.
The vendor froze under his umbrella.
A dog tried to hide in his owner's shadow.

Even the chess players under the trees
looked up from their boards
long enough to see the bronze generals

dismount and run off, leaving their horses
to peer down at the circling pigeons
who were stealing a few more crumbs from the poor.

Passivity

Tonight I turned off every light
in this stone, slate-roofed cottage,
then I walked out into the blackened woods
and sat on a rock next to a bust
of what looked like a sneering Roman consul,
a mantle of concrete draped over his shoulders.

I stared up at the ebbing quarter moon
and the stars scattered like a handful of salt
across the faraway sky,
and I visited some of my new quandaries
including where to live and what to do there,
and leaning back to take in the sizable night,

I arrived at the decision
that I would never make another decision.
Instead of darting this way or that,
I would stand at a crossroads until my watch
ran down and the clothes fell off me
and were carried by a heavy rain out to sea.

Instead of choosing one thing over another,
I would do nothing but picture
a little silver ball swinging back and forth from a cloud.

I would celebrate only the two equinoxes
and pass the rest of the time
balancing a silver scale with silver coins.

And I would see to it that the image of a seesaw—
or teeter-totter as it once was called—
was added to my family crest,
stitched into that empty patch
just below the broken plow
and above the blindfolded bee.

Ornithography

The legendary Cang Jie was said to
have invented writing after observing
the tracks of birds.

A light snow last night,
and now the earth falls open to a fresh page.

A high wind is breaking up the clouds.
Children wait for the yellow bus in a huddle,

and under the feeder, some birds
are busy writing short stories,

poems, and letters to their mothers.
A crow is working on an editorial.

That chickadee is etching a list,
and a robin walks back and forth

composing the opening to her autobiography.
All so prolific this morning,

these expressive little creatures,
and each with an alphabet of only two letters.

A far cry from me watching
in silence behind a window wondering

what just frightened them into flight—
a dog's bark, a hawk overhead?

or had they simply finished
saying whatever it was they had to say?

Baby Listening

According to the guest information directory,
baby listening is a service offered by this seaside hotel.

Baby listening—not a baby who happens to be listening,
as I thought when I first checked in.

Leave the receiver off the hook,
the directory advises,
and your infant can be monitored by the staff,

though the staff, the entry continues,
cannot be held responsible for the well-being
of the baby in question.

Fair enough, someone to listen to the baby.

But the phrase did suggest a baby who is listening,
lying there in the room next to mine
listening to my pen scratching against the page,

or a more advanced baby who has crawled
down the hallway of the hotel
and is pressing its tiny, curious ear against my door.

Lucky for some of us,
poetry is a place where both are true at once,
where meaning only one thing at a time spells
    malfunction.

Poetry wants to have the baby who is listening at my
    door
as well as the baby who is being listened to,
quietly breathing by the nearby telephone.

And it also wants the baby
who is making sounds of distress
into the curved receiver lying in the crib

while the girl at reception has just stepped out
to have a smoke with her boyfriend
in the dark by the great sway and wash of the North
    Sea.

Poetry wants that baby, too,
even a little more than it wants the others.

Bathtub Families

is not just a phrase I made up
though it would have given me pleasure
to have written those words in a notebook
then looked up at the sky wondering what they meant.

No, I saw Bathtub Families in a pharmacy
on the label of a clear plastic package
containing one cow and four calves,
a little family of animals meant to float in your tub.

I hesitated to buy it because I knew
I would then want the entire series of Bathtub Families,
which would leave no room in the tub
for the turtles, the pigs, the seals, the giraffes, and me.

It's enough just to have the words,
which alone make me even more grateful
that I was born in America
and English is my mother tongue.

I was lucky, too, that I waited
for the pharmacist to fill my prescription,
otherwise I might not have wandered
down the aisle with the Bathtub Families.

I think what I am really saying is that language
is better than reality, so it doesn't have
to be bath time for you to enjoy
all the Bathtub Families as they float in the air around
    your head.

Despair

So much gloom and doubt in our poetry—
flowers wilting on the table,
the self regarding itself in a watery mirror.

Dead leaves cover the ground,
the wind moans in the chimney,
and the tendrils of the yew tree inch toward the coffin.

I wonder what the ancient Chinese poets
would make of all this,
these shadows and empty cupboards?

Today, with the sun blazing in the trees,
my thoughts turn to the great
tenth-century celebrator of experience,

Wa-Hoo, whose delight in the smallest things
could hardly be restrained,
and to his joyous counterpart in the western provinces,
    Ye-Hah.

The Idea of Natural History at Key West

When I happened to notice myself
walking naked past a wall-length mirror

one spring morning
in a house by the water
where a friend was letting me stay,

I looked like one of those silhouettes
that illustrate the evolution of man,

but not exactly the most recent figure.
I seemed to represent a more primitive stage,
maybe not the round-shouldered ape

dragging his knuckles on the ground,
but neither the fully upright hominoid

ready to put on a suit and head for the office.
Was it something in the slope of my brow
or my slack belly?

Was this the beginning of the Great Regression
as the anthropologists of tomorrow would call it?

I was never the smartest monkey on the block,
I thought to myself in the shower,
but I was at least advanced enough to be standing

under a cascade of steaming water,
and I did have enough curiosity to wonder
what the next outline in the sequence might look like:

the man of the future stepping forward
like the others rising to their hind legs behind him,

only with a longer stride, a more ample cranium,
and maybe a set of talons,
or a pair of useless, cherubic wings.

The Fish

As soon as the elderly waiter
placed before me the fish I had ordered,
it began to stare up at me
with its one flat, iridescent eye.

I feel sorry for you, it seemed to say,
eating alone in this awful restaurant
bathed in such unkindly light
and surrounded by these dreadful murals of Sicily.

And I feel sorry for you, too—
yanked from the sea and now lying dead
next to some boiled potatoes in Pittsburgh—
I said back to the fish as I raised my fork.

And thus my dinner in an unfamiliar city
with its rivers and lighted bridges
was graced not only with chilled wine
and lemon slices but with compassion and sorrow

even after the waiter had removed my plate
with the head of the fish still staring
and the barrel vault of its delicate bones
terribly exposed, save for a shroud of parsley.

A Dog on His Master

As young as I look,
I am growing older faster than he,
seven to one
is the ratio they tend to say.

Whatever the number,
I will pass him one day
and take the lead
the way I do on our walks in the woods.

And if this ever manages
to cross his mind,
it would be the sweetest
shadow I have ever cast on snow or grass.

The Great American Poem

If this were a novel,
it would begin with a character,
a man alone on a southbound train
or a young girl on a swing by a farmhouse.

And as the pages turned, you would be told
that it was morning or the dead of night,
and I, the narrator, would describe
for you the miscellaneous clouds over the farmhouse

and what the man was wearing on the train
right down to his red tartan scarf,
and the hat he tossed onto the rack above his head,
as well as the cows sliding past his window.

Eventually—one can only read so fast—
you would learn either that the train was bearing
the man back to the place of his birth
or that he was headed into the vast unknown,

and you might just tolerate all of this
as you waited patiently for shots to ring out
in a ravine where the man was hiding
or for a tall, raven-haired woman to appear in a doorway.

But this is a poem, not a novel,
and the only characters here are you and I,
alone in an imaginary room
which will disappear after a few more lines,

leaving us no time to point guns at one another
or toss all our clothes into a roaring fireplace.
I ask you: who needs the man on the train
and who cares what his black valise contains?

We have something better than all this turbulence
lurching toward some ruinous conclusion.
I mean the sound that we will hear
as soon as I stop writing and put down this pen.

I once heard someone compare it
to the sound of crickets in a field of wheat
or, more faintly, just the wind
over that field stirring things that we will never see.

What Love Does

A fine thing, or so it sounds
on the radio in the summer
with all the windows rolled down.

Yet it pierces not only the heart
but the eyeball and the scrotum
and the little target of the nipple with arrows.

It turns everything into a symbol
like a storm that breaks loose
in the final chapter of a long novel.

And it may add sparkle to a morning,
or deepen a night
when the bed is ringed with fire.

It teaches you new joys
and new maneuvers—
the takedown, the reversal, the escape.

But mostly it comes and goes,
a bee visiting the center
of one flower, then another.

Even as the ink is drying
on her name, it is off
to visit someone in another city,

a city with two steeples,
rows of brick chimney pots,
and a school with a tree-lined entrance.

It will travel through the night to get there,
and it will arrive like an archangel
through an iron gate no one ever seemed to notice
    before.

Divorce

Once, two spoons in bed,
now tined forks

across a granite table
and the knives they have hired.

Liu Yung

This poet of the Sung dynasty is so miserable.
The wind sighs around the trees,
a single swan passes overhead,
and he is alone on the water in his skiff.

If only he appreciated life
in eleventh-century China as much as I do—
no loud cartoons on television,
no music from the ice cream truck,

just the calls of elated birds
and the steady flow of the water clock.

This Little Piggy Went to Market

is the usual thing to say when you begin
pulling on the toes of a small child,
and I have never had a problem with that.
I could easily picture the piggy with his basket
and his trotters kicking up the dust on an imaginary
     road.

What always stopped me in my tracks was
the middle toe—this little piggy ate roast beef.
I mean I enjoy a roast beef sandwich
with lettuce and tomato and a dollop of horseradish,
but I cannot see a pig ordering that in a delicatessen.

I am probably being too literal-minded here—
I am even wondering why it's called "horseradish."
I should just go along with the beautiful nonsense
of the nursery, float downstream on its waters.
After all, Little Jack Horner speaks to me deeply.

I don't want to be the one to ruin the children's party
by asking unnecessary questions about Puss in Boots
or, again, the implications of a pig eating beef.

By the way, I am completely down with going
"Wee wee wee" all the way home,
having done that many times and knowing exactly how
it feels.

Old Man Eating Alone in a Chinese Restaurant

I am glad I resisted the temptation,
if it was a temptation when I was young,
to write a poem about an old man
eating alone at a corner table in a Chinese restaurant.

I would have gotten it all wrong
thinking: the poor bastard, not a friend in the world
and with only a book for a companion.
He'll probably pay the bill out of a change purse.

So glad I waited all these decades
to record how hot and sour the hot and sour soup is
here at Chang's this afternoon
and how cold the Chinese beer in a frosted glass.

And my book—José Saramago's *Blindness*
as it turns out—is so absorbing that I look up
from its escalating horrors only
when I am stunned by one of his arresting sentences.

And I should mention the light
which falls through the big windows this time of day
italicizing everything it touches—
the plates and teapots, the immaculate tablecloths,

as well as the soft brown hair of the waitress
in the white blouse and short black skirt,
the one who is smiling now as she bears a cup of rice
and shredded beef with garlic to my favorite table in the
corner.

The Breather

Just as in the horror movies
when someone discovers that the phone calls
are coming from inside the house

so, too, I realized
that our tender overlapping
has been taking place only inside me.

All that sweetness, the love and desire—
it's just been me dialing myself
then following the ringing to another room

to find no one on the line,
well, sometimes a little breathing
but more often than not, nothing.

To think that all this time—
which would include the boat rides,
the airport embraces, and all the drinks—

it's been only me and the two telephones,
the one on the wall in the kitchen
and the extension in the darkened guestroom upstairs.

Oh, My God!

Not only in church
and nightly by their bedsides
do young girls pray these days.

Wherever they go,
prayer is woven into their talk
like a bright thread of awe.

Even at the pedestrian mall
outbursts of praise
spring unbidden from their glossy lips.

The Mortal Coil

One minute you are playing the fool,
strumming a tennis racquet as if it were a guitar
for the amusement of a few ladies
and the next minute you are lying on your deathbed,
arms stiff under the covers,
the counterpane tucked tight across your chest.

Or so seemed the progress of life
as I was flipping through the photographs
in *Proust: The Later Years* by George Painter.

Here he is at a tennis party, larking for the camera,
and 150 pages later, nothing but rictus on a pillow,
and in between, a confection dipped
into a cup of lime tea and brought to the mouth.

Which is why, instead of waiting
for our date this coming weekend,
I am now speeding to your house at 7:45 in the morning
where I hope to catch you half dressed—

and I am wondering which half
as I change lanes without looking—

with the result that we will be lifted
by the urgent pull of the flesh
into a state of ecstatic fusion, and you will be late
    for work.

And as we lie there
in the early, latticed light,
I will suggest that you take George Painter's
biography of Proust
to the office so you can show your boss
the pictures that caused you to arrive shortly
    before lunch
and he will understand perfectly,

for I imagine him to be a man of letters,
maybe even a devoted Proustian,
but at the very least a fellow creature,
ensnared with the rest of us in the same mortal coil,

or so it would appear from the wishful
vantage point of your warm and rumpled bed.

The Future

When I finally arrive there—
and it will take many days and nights—
I would like to believe others will be waiting
and might even want to know how it was.

So I will reminisce about a particular sky
or a woman in a white bathrobe
or the time I visited a narrow strait
where a famous naval battle had taken place.

Then I will spread out on a table
a large map of my world
and explain to the people of the future
in their pale garments what it was like—

how mountains rose between the valleys
and this was called geography,
how boats loaded with cargo plied the rivers
and this was known as commerce,

how the people from this pink area
crossed over into this light-green area
and set fires and killed whoever they found
and this was called history—

and they will listen, mild-eyed and silent,
as more of them arrive to join the circle,
like ripples moving toward,
not away from, a stone tossed into a pond.

Envoy

Go, little book,
out of this house and into the world,

carriage made of paper rolling toward town
bearing a single passenger
beyond the reach of this jittery pen,
far from the desk and the nosy gooseneck lamp.

It is time to decamp,
put on a jacket and venture outside,
time to be regarded by other eyes,
bound to be held in foreign hands.

So off you go, infants of the brain,
with a wave and some bits of fatherly advice:

stay out as late as you like,
don't bother to call or write,
and talk to as many strangers as you can.

acknowledgments

The author is grateful to the editors of the following journals, where some of these poems first appeared:

Alehouse: "China," "Divorce"
The Atlantic: "Searching"
Bat City Review: "Carpe Diem"
The Cortland Review: "The Golden Years"
Crazyhorse: "Aubade," "(detail)"
Five Points: "Ballistics," "High," "What Love Does"
The Florida Review: "The First Night"
Fulcrum: "Brightly Colored Boats Upturned on the Banks of the Charles," "Le Chien"
The Gettysburg Review: "New Year's Day," "Vermont, Early November"
London Review of Books: "Looking Forward," "The Poems of Others"
The Massachusetts Review: "On the Death of a Next-Door Neighbor"
Mid-American Review: "Ornithography"
New Ohio Review: "Bathtub Families"
The New York Review of Books: "Greek and Roman Statuary"
The New York Times Magazine: "The Fish"
The New Yorker: "The Future"

The Paris Review: "Tension"

Pleiades: "Addendum"

Poetry: "The Breather," "Evasive Maneuvers," "January in
Paris," "Old Man Eating Alone in a Chinese
Restaurant," "Pornography"

A Public Space: "The Lamps Unlit," "Scenes of Hell"

The Recorder: "Liu Yung"

The Southampton Review: "The Four-Moon Planet"

Subtropics: "No Things"

TriQuarterly: "Adage"

The Virginia Quarterly Review: "August," "The Great
American Poem"

West 10th: "Oh, My God"

Much gratitude is owed to many people at Random House for
bringing this book into being, especially Daniel Menaker,
David Ebershoff, and Gina Centrello. Thanks also to Shelby
White for her generous hospitality and to my family and
friends for egging me on.

about the author

BILLY COLLINS is the author of eight collections of poetry, including *The Trouble with Poetry and Other Poems, Nine Horses, Sailing Alone Around the Room, Questions About Angels, The Apple That Astonished Paris, The Art of Drowning,* and *Picnic, Lightning.* He is also the editor of *Poetry 180: A Turning Back to Poetry* and *180 More: Extraordinary Poems for Every Day.* A distinguished professor of English at Lehman College of the City University of New York, he served as Poet Laureate of the United States from 2001 to 2003 and Poet Laureate of New York State from 2004 to 2006.